Futuristics and Education

By Violet Anselmini Allain

Library of Congress Catalog Card Number: 79-89541
ISBN 0-87367-131-7
Copyright © 1979 by the Phi Delta Kappa Educational Foundation
Bloomington, Indiana

This fastback is sponsored by the Kutztown Pennsylvania Chapter of Phi Delta Kappa to commemorate the fifteenth anniversary of the founding of the chapter in 1964. The chapter made a generous contribution toward publication costs.

TABLE OF CONTENTS

Our "Future Shocked" Society

Change is one of the few certainties in today's world. Within the past three decades, some would argue that there have been as many changes in our lives as those occurring in all previously recorded history. Most people agree that the best guide to the future is the past and present. In the past, generations of families lived their lives relatively untouched by any significant change. Societies were fairly stable, and the learnings that parents had acquired were adequate for their children. Youngsters were raised to do the same kind of work their parents had done and to expect to live their adult lives in a world very similar to the one they had grown up in. Unlike the past, change now pervades nearly all aspects of our lives, and we have come to expect some degree of change during our lifetimes. Although we expect change, we sometimes experience difficulty adjusting to the accelerating rate with which it occurs.

Arnold H. Glasgow has said, "The trouble with the future is that it usually arrives before we are ready for it." This inability of people to adjust to rapid change is a malady Alvin Toffler calls "future shock." He describes it as "the dizzying disorientation brought on by the premature arrival of the future." Rapid change can be illustrated by the rate at which knowledge is being created: One-third of the items on supermarket shelves today did not exist 10 years ago; 50% of the labor force earns its living in industries that did not exist when this country was founded; 75% of all the people employed by industry 12 years from now will be producing items that have not yet been conceived of. New

7

knowledge will either extend previous knowledge or make it obsolete. Toffler relates a conversation he had with Lord James, vice-chancellor of the University of York, who said, "I took my first degree in chemistry at Oxford in 1931." Looking at the questions asked on chemistry exams at Oxford today, he continued, "I realize that not only can I not do them, but that I never could have done them, since at least two-thirds of the questions involve knowledge that simply did not exist when I graduated."

In addition to the generation of new knowledge, change is evident in our value systems. The roles of men and women in contemporary society have been altered significantly during the last decade. The consequences of the rate of change are obvious; we feel uncomfortable and uneasy in such a fast-paced world. Also, this uncontrolled acceleration of social, technological, and scientific change makes the individual feel powerless to control the future in any important way.

While earlier generations prepared their children to live in a world similar to the adults' world, today we don't know the kind of world in which our children will live. Perhaps they will have to deal with even more rapid changes than we do today. Will they be "future shocked" into a sense of helplessness and be swept along with the tide of change? Hopefully not. To help our children cope with their world, we must teach them to deal with continual change. This is one of the goals of futuristics: to teach people to function and cope with change regardless of the number of changes that may occur. Studying the future affords us the opportunity to think about and react to projected changes. It is a process by which we can anticipate, adapt to, and perhaps even feel comfortable with, change.

Since we cannot stop change, we can attempt, as Toffler suggests, to manage it.

> . . . to manage change we must anticipate it. However, the notion that one's personal future can be, to some extent, anticipated, flies in the face of persistent folk prejudice. Most people, deep down, believe that the future is a blank. Yet the truth is that we can assign probabilities to some of the changes that lie in store for us, especially certain large structural changes, and there are ways to use this knowledge in designing personal stability zones.

To learn how to manage change requires gaining a degree of control over our lives by being able to make intelligent decisions about the future from an array of possibilities. When we know how to do this, we can then avoid the confusion and anxiety caused by experiencing too much change too quickly. To cope with change requires that we eliminate the "I'll-let-tomorrow-take-care-of-itself" syndrome and become an active participant in shaping our future.

Futuristics: A New Field of Study

Futuristics, not to be confused with science fiction, is a fairly recent development. After World War II, the RAND Corporation was established as a semiprivate, nonprofit "think tank," and it became the first enduring organization primarily devoted to the systematic, ongoing study of the future. Since the 1950s, other organizations such as the Institute for the Future, the Futures Group, and the Hudson Institute have been founded to explore the array of possible futures for the U.S. and the international community through analytical and documented futures research. The futurists who work in these establishments do not use tarot cards or tea leaves to study the future but instead approach their studies scientifically and rationally.

Futuristics research is based on the assumption that human decisions now being made will shape the world. The researchers do not subscribe to the fatalistic view of an inevitable future. Harold G. Shane has indicated five aspects of futures research that differ significantly from those of conventional research:

1. Futures planning is deliberately directed by the planner's examined values and is action-oriented. It emphasizes alternative avenues rather than linear projections and concentrates on relationships among probabilities, their cross-impact upon one another, and the possible implications of such influences.
2. Futures planning is designed to point to more alternative courses of action than does conventional planning—to keep good ideas from being overlooked.

3. Traditional planning has tended to be utopian, to see tomorrow merely as an improved model of the present. Futures research recognizes the need to anticipate and to plan genuinely different concepts of the future.

4. Futures planning relies more heavily on the rational study of anticipated developments and their consequences and gives less heed to statistical analysis or projection per se.

5. In futures planning, the focus is not on the reform of the past. Rather, it concentrates on the creation of a "probabilistic environment" in which alternative consequences and possibilities are given careful study before choices are made.

The focus of futuristics, then, is the examination of future alternatives and their possible results before they are put in action. The psychological principle that anticipated change is less threatening to people than unexpected change is a critical element of futuristics. Too much unexpected change can cause one to become disoriented and to suffer from the disability that has come to be called "future shock." Through the techniques of futuristics we can learn to anticipate change and consider the consequences of a range of alternatives. Edward Cornish has defined futuristics as:

> A field of activity that seeks to identify, analyze, and evaluate possible future changes in human life and the world. The word implies a rational rather than mystical approach to the future, but also accepts artistic, imaginative, and experiential approaches as offering contributions that can be useful and valid.

So we can speak of futuristics as providing an organized study of the future utilizing a wide range of disciplines.

During the last 10 years, attitudes about the future have been changing. For one thing, we are thinking more about what we might make happen and the things we need to do to create a better future world rather than passively accepting a fixed, predetermined world. Also, through a variety of techniques, we believe that it is possible to study the future.

Specifically, what does this mean for education? Futuristics can aid in sensitizing the educational policy maker to alternative futures that will require skilled leadership. But on a more basic level, futures research for education attempts to deal with the question, "What kind of education will best prepare students for the world in which they will live their adult lives?" In partial response to this question, a variety of future-oriented courses have been generated. By 1973 approximately 400 colleges and universities included such offerings in their curricula. Since the 1966-67 school year, when Priscilla Griffiths offered a future studies course at Melbourne High School in Florida, a growing number of elementary and secondary schools have added such courses to their programs. Much of the important research in educational futures has been developed by the Educational Policy Research Center at the Stanford Research Institute and by the Syracuse University Research Corporation.

The implicit message in the above developments points to an increased concern for and about the future. Since our society is undergoing convulsive change and experiencing many crises, greater attention must be directed to the future. Also, if schools are to prepare youth for the future, then a future-oriented curriculum would help achieve this purpose. It would emphasize the future society in which students will live as adults. It would also train students to cope with change, that is, teach them how to be psychologically prepared to adjust to a society experiencing a continuing rapid rate of change. In light of this, it calls for educating youth with a heightened future consciousness.

If the schools do not prepare children for the probabilities of the future, the schools are doing students a great disservice. Charles Kettering once said, "My interest is in the future, because I am going to spend the rest of my life there." How true this is, especially for the school-children of today who will spend most of their adult lives in the twenty-first century. We assume that the kinds of things students learn today will, hopefully, be of some benefit to them in the future. But too often, what one studies in school is obsolete by the time one reaches adulthood. Nowhere is this more evident than in the fields of science and technology.

With our society in a state of flux as a result of new knowledge being discovered at alarming rates and human values shifting and changing, we know for certain that our future society will be very different from what it is today. Therefore, it is questionable policy to base education solely on the past. Preparing for a new society also deserves appropriate consideration in the curriculum. This future-oriented approach would emphasize the teaching of skills and topics that students can use to meet the challenges ahead. The future is made up of predictable and unpredictable tomorrows, and we must give children an insight into the problems and opportunities they may face.

Futurists contend that students need to be taught certain new "basics" in order to prepare them for adult life. One of these basics is the ability to gather information about important future possibilities. Intelligent decisions about the future cannot be made in a vacuum. If individuals are to make thoughtful choices about their futures, then they must have opportunities to collect pertinent information about the variety of possible futures. One other basic futurists view as essential is the skill to anticipate effectively. The ability to consider the effects of actions is necessary if people are to develop the habit of future-oriented thinking.

Acquiring skills in these areas can be easily integrated into existing programs. Techniques such as polling, forecasting, and analyzing trends can supply information about potential futures. Scenario writing and studying science fiction can encourage students to think more imaginatively about the future and to anticipate the future consequences of past and present actions. These teaching methods will be discussed in more detail later in this fastback. Such techniques and content can foster both long-range and open-ended attitudes in students' thinking concerning the future—their future.

Conceptions of the Future: Optimistic Vs. Pessimistic

An interesting exercise is to ask your students to write down their conceptions of the future. It has been this writer's experience that the responses range from the pessimistic to the optimistic and usually include a large dose of *Star Wars* mentality. Reactions include: "the unknown," "an unknown mystery that awaits for me," "that which is to come," "the world being in turmoil," "change, computers, confusion," "progress," "new technological gains and a better understanding of different people," "trouble; all the new technology is creating more problems in the world," "computers ruling the world," and "humans inhabiting other planets." One student who obviously had one eye on global concerns and the other on her personal goals wrote the intriguing but rather unsettling statement, ". . . certainly not world peace but a lot more wars and famine and two years of school to go." This simple exercise points to the fact that concepts of the future are often vague and ambiguous.

Alvin Toffler has noted that people frequently have personal plans that are incongruent with a projected future. For example, one 15-year-old student predicted such events as a cancer cure, a U.S.-USSR alliance against China, test tube babies, an accidental nuclear explosion, the spread of terrorism, and robot computers. But her personal forecast included getting her own apartment, attending school in interior design, getting a driver's license, getting a dog, getting married, having children, and dying. Thus, the world events she listed seemed to have little impact upon her personal life and illustrates the attitude of many that the future is something that happens to somebody else.

Speculation about the future and what it holds for us has always been a favorite diversion for some people. Some of these predictions have been quite accurate, as when H. G. Wells prophesied the emergence of sprawling megalopolises and space exploration. Others have suffered from myopia. For instance, at the turn of this century, magazine writer Ray Stannard Baker predicted, "Automobiles will replace the crashing of horses' hoofs, making city streets almost as quiet as a country lane and far less crowded." Another example of faulty forecasting occurred when a committee was organized in 1486 by King Ferdinand and Queen Isabella of Spain to study Columbus's plans to sail west to find a shorter route to the East Indies. In 1490 the committee reported that a voyage such as Columbus contemplated was impossible because:

> 1) A voyage to Asia would require three years. 2) The Western Ocean is infinite and perhaps unnavigable. 3) If he reached the Antipodes (the land on the other side of the globe from Europe), he could not get back. 4) There are no Antipodes because the greater part of the globe is covered with water, and because Saint Augustine says so. . . . 5) Of the five zones, only three are habitable. 6) So many centuries after the Creation it was unlikely that anyone could find hitherto unknown lands of any value.

In a more recent case, the noted scientist Vannevar Bush gave this advice to President Truman in 1945 about the atomic bomb: "The bomb will never go off, and I speak as an expert in explosives." Obviously, predictions can be made about the future, but these are fruitless exercises unless we make a serious attempt to understand the future in terms of present developments that can have various consequences. And this is what futures research attempts to do.

The future can be viewed optimistically—a blind faith in continuous progress—or it can be viewed pessimistically—due to world crises that seem insolvable. The first scenario is presented by Herman Kahn in *The Next 200 Years.* Kahn claims that we will overcome our pressing problems through technological innovations. This "techno-fix" attitude forecasts that life will continue in the future much as it is today, except that more people will benefit from the results of technological progress. The second scenario takes the position that the quality of life will deteriorate due to the depletion of the earth's resources. This viewpoint is found in *The Limits to Growth* by Donella H. Meadows et al., and is summarized by a 1969 quote from that work by the late U Thant.

> I do not wish to seem overdramatic, but I can only conclude from the information that is available to me as Secretary-General, that the members of the United Nations have perhaps ten years left in which to subordinate their ancient quarrels and launch a global partnership to curb the arms race, to improve the human environment, to defuse the population explosion, and to supply the required momentum to development efforts. If such global partnership is not forged within the next decade, then I very much fear that the problems I have mentioned will have reached such staggering proportions that they will be beyond our capacity to control.

Viewing the world from either extreme isn't healthy. Certainly there is good reason for alarm, but there are also developments that allow some hope for the future.

Futurism attempts to maintain this balanced approach. This balanced perspective should serve as a guide as we prepare to teach the skills and knowledge that individuals will need for a future society that is becoming more complex and as we attempt to instill the attitude that one can influence and change the future in desirable directions.

Focusing on the Future

Whether students learn how to dissect a frog, divide two mixed fractions, diagram sentences, type a business letter, or paint a picture, we assume that these skills, along with the countless other things they learn in school, will serve some useful purpose in the future. This notion fails to take into account how our rapidly changing society will affect the youth of today. Toffler has said, "All education springs from some image of the future. If the image of the future held by society is grossly inaccurate, its education system will betray its youth." We do our students a great disservice if we provide them with a curriculum that emphasizes only the past or only one version of the future.

Providing children with a future-oriented curriculum should help them to develop their thinking about a variety of alternative futures. Basic to the notion of alternative futures is the idea that one can choose from an array of options and that the choices made will have some impact in shaping the future. In other words, we can determine within limits the kind of future we want. On the other hand, if individuals have a very restricted view of the future and believe that they have little control over it, then they are likely to feel that choices made today have little significance. Therefore, a person's image of the future will have an influence on his decision-making capacity.

We all make certain assumptions about the future. These may be short-term, for instance, the plans we have for this afternoon or tomorrow; or, they may be long-term, as in our career designs over the next five, 10, or 15 years. All of these factors together constitute our image of the future. If we have a narrow outlook about the future, then we are not likely to see much relationship between present actions and future possibilities. People's image of the future can have an important effect on what they do right now. Research indicates that students' perception of the future plays a major role in their performance in school. If they expect to be employed in a low-status occupation, then they will see little relationship between what they do in school and their careers. A future-oriented perspective can provide the motivation for achievement.

Thinking about and imagining our roles in the future is called the future-focused role-image. Benjamin D. Singer states, "The future-focused role-image is our self-image projected into the future and it lends meaning to much of what we do in the present." Those who cannot project themselves into the future can only respond to the immediacy of the present and are unable to envision an array of possible futures. The development of future-focused role-images is necessary in order to establish personal goals that an individual can work toward achieving.

The lack of a future-focused role-image is often seen in minority groups where the children have a very restricted view of future possibilities. Difficulty in developing a future-oriented perspective for minorities probably stems from their lack of confidence in future rewards. Minority students have no guarantee that obtaining a proper education will assure them a job. This has been a chronic problem with minorities and has resulted in a distrustful attitude toward a society that confers future rewards inconsistently and discriminatorily. This also makes it hard to teach minority students to work in the present toward some future goal.

For many people, the future is too far away and unpredictable; consequently, delayed rewards serve no useful purpose. It is the present that is real to them; the future is too distant to be concerned about. This situation is underscored by the common attitude among minorities that they have very little, if any, control over their future. Adolescent blacks more frequently than whites believe that factors external to themselves determine the future; that is, what they do now has very little impact upon their future. Also, many black adolescents believe that if they want to achieve their goals, they most likely will have to use tactics not approved of by society. For example, when young Harlem boys were asked how people managed to become rich, they responded that these people had done so either through illegitimate means or good luck. It is this feeling of powerlessness over one's destiny and the historical undependability of future rewards that operate against minority children developing positive and fulfilling future-focused role-images.

Women are another group for whom the variety of future-focused role-images is limited. Traditional roles of houseworker and child-bearer or sex-stereotyped occupational roles such as teacher, nurse, or secretary are still the most prevalent ones presented to female children in our culture. Pauline B. Bart, in her article, "Why Women See the Future Differently from Men," contends that, "The failure to encourage independence and to widen the range of possibilities open to women produces a fatalism and passivity that flies in the face of all the educational rhetoric about producing resourceful, self-reliant, and hope-filled people for tomorrow."

Recent societal trends point to the fact that the role of women is changing. For example, the number of women holding jobs has grown from 18 million in 1950 to 42.1 million in 1978, a 129% increase. Currently women account for 42% of the U.S. work force. Although these figures are impressive, we must also take into consideration that nearly 80% of these working women are in clerical, sales, service, and factory jobs that are typically low-paying positions. For example, on the average, women who worked full time in 1977 earned 59 cents for every dollar earned by men. There are many reasons for this situation, but one cannot ignore the influential role that future images play in shaping one's destiny. If young girls are given a limited view of their capabilities and opportunities, then they can be easily channeled into jobs that provide low economic returns. The women's movement, in part, has addressed this issue and has brought about some modest changes in societal expectations and educational practices that have increased the career options open to women.

For education to have any relevance at all for young people, they should feel that they will have meaningful roles in society as adults. Sex-role stereotyping and racial and ethnic prejudice operate against the goal of fair treatment of the sexes and minorities and constrict these children's notions of their future-focused role-images. Education should seek to improve the images children have about the future and their place in it. A future-oriented curriculum would help achieve this end by encouraging youngsters to think more creatively about their future possibilities.

Alternative Futures:
Possible, Probable, Preferable

The concept of alternative futures is fundamental to futuristics. People generally conceptualize the future as being inevitable, which means that there is one, static future somewhere off in the distance. Futurists explicitly point out that there is a variety of futures, not one single future. These alternative futures are dependent on several factors: history, that is, past events and trends that have an influence on the future; chance, the occurrences we are unable to plan for; and human choice, the decisions we make that affect the future. It is important to understand that futurists do not claim to predict the future; rather they attempt to heighten our awareness of the range of alternative futures that might come about and of the role that history, chance, and human choice might play in influencing positively or negatively any specific future.

Futurist Draper L. Kauffman, Jr. speaks of the future as a "zone of potentiality" rather than "that which is going to happen" and that any "knowledge about the future" is seen as "knowledge about what is possible." In this way, one thinks in terms of future possibilities and alternatives rather than what is certain or inevitable. These perspectives can best be illustrated by two metaphors. One can view life as a long roller coaster ride and the future as the track upon which it rides. We are unable to see all the twists and turns of the track in advance and can only see each part as we come to it. We cannot change the course of the ride or even get off when we want. We are a captive to this experience and can do little about a future that is fixed. Another view characterizes the future as a great ocean on which we are navigating a ship. There are many destinations that we may sail toward. While navigating, we take into consideration such factors as the currents, weather conditions, and unfamiliar waters in order to reach our destination safely. The first metaphor views the future as determined by our circumstances and there is not much we can do to change or alter it. Futurists reject this notion and opt instead for the second metaphor, which claims that by using foresight, one is able to determine, to some extent, one's future.

The alternative futures approach requires the use of several skills that can be developed through the techniques cited in the next section of this fastback. First, one must learn to think more imaginatively about the future in order to avoid the single future trap. This often necessitates scrutinizing previous notions of the future and restructuring them to fit the more flexible perspective of a future as something to be created or invented. Second, one must evaluate the impact of possible futures. Reflecting upon the effects of certain actions is essential when considering future possibilities. We must not only be aware of alternative courses of action that are open to us, but we must also choose wisely from among them. This process raises basic questions of what is *possible*, what is *probable*, and above all, what is *preferable*. Alvin Toffler notes:

> Every society faces not merely a succession of *probable* futures, but an array of *possible* futures, and a conflict over *preferable* futures. The management of change is the effort to convert certain possibles into probables, in pursuit of agreed-on preferables.

So we can look ahead to an array of possible futures, of which some are more likely to occur than others. With this in mind, we can choose the most desirable future and then take the steps to reach it. It is this perspective that would disclaim the inevitability of a single future and allow us greater control of our destiny.

Futuristic Investigation

I hope that by now I have convinced you that future studies belong in the school curriculum. If you agree but are rather puzzled as to how to begin to implement a program, below are some of the techniques that can be used in teaching about the future. This is not meant to be an exhaustive list, but instead to highlight those methods that have been used with some degree of success. Most of these techniques can be geared to elementary, secondary, or university students. There are several books and articles that can be helpful to teachers: *Teaching Tomorrow Today,* by Ronald T. LaConte; *Teaching the Future,* by Draper L. Kauffman, Jr.; and "The Current Methods of Futures Research," an article by Theodore J. Gordon published in *The Futurists,* edited by Alvin Toffler.

Methods for future studies attempt to help students develop a more flexible attitude toward the future and think more imaginatively about it. The exercises cited here are excellent for promoting discussion about future possibilities, a topic basic to any future-oriented approach.

Scenarios

A scenario is a "future history," a narrative that describes a possible series of events that might lead to some future state of affairs. This fictionalized forecast is written from the point of view of a specific future date, such as 50 or 100 years hence. It describes the events that occurred from the present up to that date. In writing a scenario, one attempts to construct a logical sequence of events leading from the present, or any other given time, to a future condition. The possibility that these events will occur is usually derived from analyzing present trends or the consensus of expert opinion. For instance, we can develop a scenario for the year 2000 by using the population trends cited below:

1. The population of the U.S. will increase from its present level of about 218 million to approximately 262.5 million by the year 2000 if the growth rate of 0.8% a year stays about the same.
2. The predominant group will be composed of the individuals born between 1945 and 1965 who will be from 35 to 55 years old by the year 2000.
3. There will be great growth in the number of people over 65 years of age who will live longer.

Based on this information, we could write a scenario that takes place in 2000. It might look back over the last two decades and recount the changes in the American lifestyle that now emphasizes middle and old age rather than youth, since a majority of people are in the older age bracket. It might also discuss the tremendous growth of government-financed services for the aged caused by the shifts in our population and the other possible demands made by this age group, such as raising the retirement age to 80.

By using a variety of data, a scenario writer can make a persuasive case for the probability of a particular series of events to occur. In the scenario "Eco-Catastrophe!," Paul Ehrlich forecasts the death of the ocean.

> The end of the ocean came late in the summer of 1979, and it came even more rapidly than the biologists had expected. There had even been signs for more than a decade, commencing with the discovery in 1968 that DDT slows down photosynthesis in marine plant life. It was announced in a short paper in the technical journal, *Science*, but to ecologists it smacked of doomsday. They knew that all life in the sea depends on photosynthesis, the chemical process by which green plants bind the sun's energy and make it available to living things. And they knew that DDT and similar chlorinated hydrocarbons had polluted the entire surface of the earth, including the sea.

This scenario, which was written in 1969, makes a projection of the end of the ocean based upon the expert opinion of ecologists and the discovery of the relationship between DDT and photosynthesis.

Used in the classroom, scenario writing aids students to think more imaginatively about the future and to explore future possibilities of past and present trends. The following activities will help students in scenario writing.

Headlines: With younger students, supply newspaper headlines that might appear in the year 2025, such as, **CARS BANNED FROM STREETS AND HIGHWAYS,** or **NEW LAW SAYS PEOPLE OVER 35 MUST BE "ELIMINATED,"** or **LAST DROP OF GASOLINE SOLD TO THE PRESIDENT OF U.S.** Then ask students to write the newspaper article to match the headline. They should take into account the factors that led up to such drastic news items. Of course, students could create their own headlines and articles for a future date or even compose the entire newspaper as a group project complete with advertisements, television listings, advice columns, editorials, sports pages, weather reports, and classified ads. This activity can illustrate the variety of alternative futures open to us and the consequences we may suffer due to decisions that are being made in the present.

Autobiographies: Along these same lines, students could write several autobiographies looking back over a period of 50 or 75 years. Each of these autobiographies should be based on a different scenario for society as a whole and the events in the person's life should reflect this. As a variation of this exercise, ask students to write their own obituaries.

Brainstorming: A more involved approach could entail a brainstorming session in which the entire class lists a variety of events that might occur within the next 50 or 100 years. Each of these events could be classified into topics such as science/technology, government, population, energy, work, lifestyle, global affairs, etc. The next step would be to divide each of these future events among groups of students. It is then the task of the group to develop a scenario with the assigned possibilities.

An important follow-up for any scenario writing exercise is that scenarios should be shared with the class and analyzed. Below are some pertinent questions suggested by Kauffman:

1. Which of these scenarios do you think the most plausible?
2. Which do you think are the most unlikely?
3. Do any of these scenarios fit the image of the future that you had before this exercise?
4. What are your own personal plans for the future?
5. How well do those plans fit into each of these different scenarios?

Science Fiction

Frank Herbert, in *The Wounded Planet,* wrote:

> Right up there with the loudest was our little band of science fiction writers, a hardy, resourceful, and imaginative lot, saying: "Here are a few of the possible hells, a few of the possible ends, and some colorful alternatives."
>
> Our batting average has been frighteningly high.

The accuracy with which some science fiction writers have been able to describe our future world cannot be ignored. And for this reason, a study of science fiction is an integral part of any future-oriented curriculum. When using science fiction in this way, it is not studied as a particular genre of literature but rather as examples of possible alternative futures. The primary concern is to present a variety of imaginative, thoughtful, and, perhaps, alarming views of the future. Science fiction can help us to anticipate change in our own world more readily.

There are several different kinds of science fiction. Some science fiction, like that of Flash Gordon or *Star Wars,* deals chiefly with the adventures of a particular hero. Actually, the plots of these adventures could have taken place in the Old West as well as on a spaceship, but different gadgetry is used. This is the kind of writing that first attracts the young reader, along with encounters with alien beings. The kind of science fiction that should be stressed in a futuristics class might better be called social science fiction. The emphasis in this type of writing is on how people cope with a situation in the context of the future. Much of this writing explores the sequence of events that led up to the ethical and social problems produced by technological and scientific developments. For example, in Aldous Huxley's *Brave New World* where embryos are grown artificially so that people can be genetically designed to fit society's needs, we find a culture that is static and uniform. This book sparks lively discussions of values, politics, and individual freedom and raises questions about the direction in which our society is heading.

Bernard C. Hollister and Deane C. Thompson in their book, *Grokking the Future,* have developed some very creative lessons for using works of science fiction effectively in the classroom. They suggest the following questions to elicit student response:

Economic: What is considered wealth in this society? Who produces and who consumes products?

Political: How is order kept in the society? Who has the power? What allowance is made for the deviant or nonconformist? What sort of leader is considered "good"? What role does the military play? What would pose the greatest threat to the society? Why? What is the author's conception of man: Is man basically good? Bad? Trustworthy?

Social: What classes exist? How does one gain and lose status? Is status ascribed or achieved? In other words, does one gain status by birth or can one work his way up? How difficult is it to move from one class to another? What is the place of the family?

Religious: What religious beliefs prevail? What is the role of a supernatural being? How is the religion organized? Who holds the most religious power in the society?

Artistic: Is any allowance made for artistic and aesthetic expression? What kinds of art, music, literature, if any, exist in society? What role does the government play in controlling artistic and aesthetic expression?

Other
Cultures: How does the society view other societies? Suspiciously?

General: How would you like living in this particular society? What would you find most distasteful about it? What would you find most enjoyable about it? If you could change one thing in the society, what would you change and why? What would pose the greatest threat to the society? Why? To what

extent do you see present-day American society in the story?
What would have to specifically happen for American society to become like the story? How might this be prevented?

To motivate students to think about future worlds, one can ask
"what if . . ." questions. The variety of these questions is endless. For
example, one could ask:

What if . . . teachers were replaced by machines?
there were no more trees left?
everyone had his own robot?
you had a friend that lived on Mars?
cars, trucks, and buses were outlawed?
there were telephones where you could see the person you
were talking to?
every home had a computer?
everyone lived to be over 100 years old?
you could take a pill to make you smart?
people could no longer have children?

Also, students may want to do their own science fiction writing by in-
venting their own planet. What is life like there? How is it governed?
What natural resources are available? What problems does it have?
How is it different from our existing society?

Science fiction is like an elaborate scenario in that it helps us to be
more future-oriented and more imaginative about possible future
worlds and the changes they will bring.

Group Opinion

Depending on one expert to predict future events can be very dan-
gerous. Kauffman suggests that methods other than the projections of
a single authority can be utilized to gain some insight into the future.
He recommends the use of commissions, polls, and the Delphi technique.

A commission is a committee of experts that is brought together to
discuss an issue in a face-to-face confrontation in order to arrive at
some consensus. This method has an advantage over the single expert
model in that ideas will be thoroughly scrutinized and debated before
they are accepted by the group. The major disadvantage is that some

individuals may dominate the discussion by virtue of their personality or reputation rather than by the merit of their argument.

Polls are used to obtain a summary of expert opinion. The respondents answer questions about the probability, preferability, or impact of an array of possible future events. This method avoids the influence of a strong personality or established reputation, which is the weakness of commissions. But polls lack the major advantage of experts interacting with other experts. Here the people being questioned can only give their views and there is no opportunity to react to the views of others. Polls gather information about what people think and therefore are useful as a classroom teaching technique. By developing appropriate questions about the next 10, 25, or 50 years and surveying various groups in the community (business people, homemakers, politicians, teachers, students, administrators, etc.), students can determine what changes people expect in the future and their attitudes toward them.

The Delphi technique attempts to combine the advantages of commissions and polls. It seeks a consensus of experts by having their opinions anonymously filtered through an intermediary. Theodore J. Gordon describes the technique as follows:

> Anonymity exists at two levels; not only are participants unknown to each other, but the individual responses are never attributed to particular respondents. In the first round of a typical Delphi study, the participants might be asked when a future event might take place. Their answers would be collated by the experimenters and fed back to them in a second round. The second-round questionnaire would seek justification of extreme views expressed in round 1. The responses would again be collated by the experimenters and furnished to the participants in a third (and usually final) round. This questionnaire would ask that the experts reassess their previous positions in view of those taken by the other participants.

A classroom exercise of the Delphi technique can be accomplished in a similar manner to that of the survey example used above. The only difference is that respondents would be given feedback from the other participants and the process would be repeated several times. The purpose of the Delphi technique is not to find out what *will* happen, but to provide a fairly reliable indicator of a consensus opinion of what *might* happen.

Cross-Impact Matrix

The cross-impact matrix technique is a method that uses the square grid pattern of a matrix to analyze the interrelationships between events and developments. It operates under the assumption that most events and trends are in some way connected with other events and trends. To assess the impact that a number of factors will have on each other will give us additional information on how the future is shaped from these interactions. Some versions of this method require complicated mathematical computations, but simpler procedures can also afford one the opportunity of analyzing various forces in terms of their impact on each other.

	A	B	C
A	1) X	2) AB	3) AC
B	4) BA	5) X	6) BC
C	7) CA	8) CB	9) X

Fig. 1. Basic matrix

30

The most basic type of matrix uses a table on which a number of factors are listed along the top edge horizontally and the same factors are listed on the left side vertically. In Figure 1 we can see the forces (A, B, C) listed on the top and on the left. The points of interaction are analyzed to determine the impact one force has on another force. For example square 2 is the intersection at which factor A has an impact on factor B (AB). Square 3 highlights the impact A exerts on factor C (AC). The matrix would be systematically analyzed in this fashion until the entire grid is completed.

A cross-impact matrix has been used on the elementary school level by Jerry Glenn and Cindy Guy. They asked fifth-graders to select three of their favorite activities. The students put these activities in matrix form and attempted to determine how each activity would affect the others at the point of interaction. Figure 2 illustrates the cross-impact matrix developed by one of the students in which she listed the recreational goals of travel and swimming and examined how they affected each other as well as her educational goal of going to college. Such an exercise can help students to determine their priorities and clarify their

How will this affect this?	I want to travel.	I want to swim better.	I want to go to college.
I want to travel.	**X**	I might not be near a swimming pool.	If I travel, I might not have time to go to college.
I want to swim better.	I might not be able to travel because of workouts and swim meets.	**X**	I might have to go to swim meets during college.
I want to go to college.	If I go to college, I might not have time to travel.	I might have too much work to have time to swim.	**X**

Fig. 2. Cross-impact matrix of recreational goals

goals. It also highlights those activities that may be compatible or in conflict with one another.

A more sophisticated version of a cross-impact matrix uses major problem areas such as population, energy, science/technology, international relations, and lifestyle and develops possible trends within these. Then these trends are analyzed according to the strength (strong, weak, no impact) and the direction (positive or negative) of each cross impact. This kind of matrix is illustrated in Figure 3, where the problem areas are listed at the top and left side of the matrix with the possible trends listed under areas on the left side. Each of the entries (a or b) in the individual boxes of the grid represents the impact of one of the possible trends on one of the general problem areas. The impact may be designated as strong negative (--), moderate negative (-), no signifi-

	1 Population	2 Energy	3 Science/ Technology	4 International Relations	5 Lifestyle
1. Population a. Expanded use of birth control tech- niques b. Extended life span	1. **X**	2. a. (++) b. (--)	3. a. (+) b. (+)	4. a. (+) b. (0)	5. a. (++) b. (-)
2. Energy a. Avoidance of fossil fuels b. More expensive	6. a. (0) b. (--)	7. **X**	8. a. (++) b. (++)	9. a. (+) b. (-)	10. a. (-) b. (--)
3. Science/Technology a. Genetic engineering b. Electronic revolu- tion will continue	11. a. (+) b. (+)	12. a. (+) b. (+)	13. **X**	14. a. (+) b. (+)	15. a. (+) b. (+)
4. International Relations a. World government established b. Third world nations more powerful	16. a. (+) b. (-)	17. a. (+) b. (--)	18. a. (0) b. (+)	19. **X**	20. a. (+) b. (-)
5. Lifestyle a. Greater mobility b. Greater economic independence of women	21. a. (-) b. (+)	22. a. (--) b. (0)	23. a. (0) b. (+)	24. a. (0) b. (+)	25. **X**

Fig. 3. Cross-impact matrix of major problem areas

cant impact (0), moderate positive (+), and strong positive (++). The completed matrix in this figure represents the work of graduate students who were enrolled in the writer's futuristics class. We first identified the problem areas and then two trends that, through our research, seemed to be prevalent. It should be noted that this exercise could become more involved with the addition of other problem areas and three, four, or five trends for each. Some of the trends we identified were:

1. Population:
   a. Through the use of contraceptives, birth control is affecting the population by slowing down the birth rate.
   b. Medical research has been able to prolong one's life span, which is evident by the growth of the over-65 population group.
2. Energy:
   a. Due to limited energy-producing resources, alternatives such as nulcear energy or energy from natural sources (sunlight, geo-thermal, water, and wind) are being researched.
   b. Because of our reliance on imported oil, we have very little control over its price. The cost of developing new sources of domestic oil is passed on to the consumer.
3. Science/Technology:
   a. Scientific discoveries will enable people to determine the genetic make-up of their children.
   b. Computers and electronic gadgetry will continue to expand and become available for private use at relatively low cost.
4. International Relations:
   a. A world government will be established in order to provide a more equitable distribution of the earth's resources.
   b. The Third World countries will be in a very powerful bargaining position due to their vast natural resources, which will be in great demand.
5. Lifestyle:
   a. The trend of families moving more frequently will continue.
   b. More women will continue to enter the work force and remain there for a longer period of time.

We then went through the individual squares of the matrix and analyzed the strength and direction of the impact for each trend under every problem area. For instance, it was determined that the first population trend concerning expanded use of birth control techniques would have a strong positive impact on energy since a reduced birth rate would help to decrease energy consumption. Science/technology and international relations shared a moderately positive impact with this trend since more scientific research is being generated in this area and a decreasing world population would help solve some of the global problems of poverty and food shortages. Lifestyle had a strong positive impact with this population trend since as a result of the widespread use of birth control, adults now have a greater degree of choice in deciding when, if at all, to have children. Birth control also affords them increased mobility and independence.

The second population trend, an increase in life span, has a strong negative impact for energy because the increase means a greater demand for limited resources. This trend would interact moderately positively with science/technology since medical science, which is helping to prolong life, will continue to be supported. No significant impact of this trend was designated for international relations, but it did have a moderately negative impact on lifestyle due to the additional burdens caused by caring for one or several older members of a family.

It is important to understand that a matrix such as this does not provide any definitive answers, but it serves the purpose of raising questions and generating discussion about the interrelatedness of events and how they may affect one another.

Simulation Gaming

Simulations are based on the creation of an artificial environment where the researcher manipulates variables within this environment to observe the results. Some simulations can be mechanical, such as the use of model ships and submarines by the U.S. Navy to examine their performance in a model ocean. Other simulations are mathematical and may require the use of a computer. Simulation games, on the other hand, are exercises where participants interact in a certain environment. This technique is very appropriate for classroom use since it helps students to understand an unfamiliar situation and determine how to operate in it. Usually students are asked to role play and make decisions that often require debate, argument, stating cases, and attempting to persuade others. Through simulation gaming, students learn about the issues under study and gain a better understanding of other points of view. (See Phi Delta Kappa's fastback No. 54, *Simulation Games for the Classroom* by Mark Heyman.)

Simulation games provide individuals with an opportunity to learn about situations that cannot be experienced directly. And since we cannot directly experience the future, this technique is ideally suited for futuristics. In this area, simulation games are used to give students an insight into future situations they may experience or a chance to make choices concerning future planning in which a variety of factors must be considered. For example, Ronald T. LaConte in *Teaching Tomorrow Today* suggests "The Neighborhood Game," which takes about two class periods to complete. The directions follow:

Divide into groups of between five and 10 members. Each group is to consider itself a neighborhood. Decide on a set of rules by which your neighborhood will live. For example, will you allow apartment houses? Will you allow any use of drugs? Will you allow cars, trucks, and buses within the neighborhood? Will you have one large shopping center or many small shops? Will you have a large community garden or will each house have its own? Assume that the neighborhood will have no fewer than 500 and no more than 2,000 residents. If some members of the group disagree with the majority decisions and feel that they could not live in such a neighborhood, they should move to another group. Once a group has a complete set of rules, they should post these on a chair back so that anyone in search of a new neighborhood can see what each one will be like. (This should take one class period.)

At the beginning of the second class period, each group should appoint a spokesperson who will have between two and five minutes to try to sell his/her neighborhood to any uncommitted class members. At the end of these speeches anyone (whether or not a member of one of the groups) may shift groups. Once everyone has chosen some neighborhood, the winning group will be considered to be the one with the most members.

In this simulation game, the students must decide the kind of neighborhood they wish to develop and in doing so they must consider the consequences of the rules they establish. For instance, they may decide to ban cars, trucks, and buses within the boundaries of their neighborhood for the purposes of reducing pollution. But this arrangement may not attract other class members unless some provision is made for alternative means of transportation. Students may learn that the obvious solution to a problem may have some complicated consequences and, therefore, not be as simple as anticipated—a very important lesson indeed.

The above techniques are merely jumping-off points for the creative teacher to use in the classroom in order to expand students' conceptions and imagination about the future.

Futuristics in the Classroom: Selected Examples

There is a variety of ways futuristics can be incorporated into the curriculum that can lead students to a heightened future consciousness. Future studies can be offered as a separate course or integrated into existing courses. The future is an area of study that is relevant to all educational levels. Below are a few examples of how it can be implemented. Some of these have been noted by James Stirewalt in the *World Future Society Bulletin*.

Elementary Schools

Fort Myer Elementary School in Arlington, Virginia, has a program called "Projecting for the Future" (PFF) consisting of a variety of electives that are taught every Wednesday for seven weeks. The program is designed to provide students with an orientation to their alternative futures, to increase their awareness of potential careers, and to help them gain new interests in the use of leisure time (an aspect of life that may become increasingly important in the future society). A futures council, which includes students, parents, teachers, the principal, and outside resource people, develops each seven-week program. Recent subjects included aerospace alternatives, communications, international relations, energy futures, social problems, multi-ethnic cultures, career education, leisure activities, movie making, and others.

"Thinking the Future" was a futures program at Wallings Road

Elementary School in Brecksville, Ohio. It consisted of a series of three to four short courses held throughout the 1972-73 school year. Classes grouped at the K through 2, 3 through 4, and 5 through 6 grade-levels met for an hour a day twice a week over a five-week period. Students were involved in individual or group projects. One group, for example, interviewed residents of a neighborhood to find out how the area had changed over a period of time and what additional changes the residents anticipated.

"Spaceship Earth" involved 80 sixth-graders at John Tyler Elementary School in Alexandria, Virginia. The youngsters transformed their classroom into an imaginary Spaceship Earth and attempted to create an environment in which all their learning needs could be satisfied during an interstellar journey. Among other projects, several students created a planetarium in a tent, the inside of which was covered with star charts and contained a model of the Apollo 12 capsule.

Secondary Schools

A recent interdisciplinary team-taught course in futuristics at Port Huron Northern High School in Port Huron, Michigan, focused on land use, ecology, and global concepts of the future, using case studies, simulations, and field trips as well as readings and films. Students then applied their knowledge by working on actual land use problems in the Port Huron area. In studying the nature of rapid change and the need for adaptability, the students read Edward Bellamy's *Looking Backward* and George Orwell's *1984* and discussed such topics as cities of the future, computers and cybernation, and genetic engineering, including the possibilities of cloning, test tube babies, and cryogenics. To explore the question of how humans use land, the students looked at slides showing how land is used in the city of Port Huron and the surrounding county. To understand the problems of city planning, the students played the *New Town* game and *Locating a Plant Locally* simulation.

"Futuristics: Theory and Application" is a year-long course in the high schools of Richfield and Burnsville, Minnesota, which consists of two major parts: 1) an introduction to theoretical futuristics in which students study the ideas of futurists and the nature of a complex modern society, and 2) an independent project in which each student researches the future of a specific interest area such as genetics, aerospace, or the family.

A course in futuristics is offered at Scotia High School in Scotia, New York. Its primary objective is not predicting the future but rather discussing possibilities and how future society will adapt and learn to control what the future might bring. The course covers English, geometry, physics, history, religion, economics, and other subjects. Students read science fiction and write scenarios that project themselves into future situations.

Colleges/Universities

"Colloquium on the Future" is a course offered at Ball State University in Muncie, Indiana, and covers the subjects of business, architecture and planning, education, nursing, library science, industrial education and technology, and home economics, among others. Its syllabus states that the colloquium is concerned with:

1. Images we hold of the future and how those images influence our decisions and actions today;
2. Facts about the present, how we got here, and where we appear to be headed in the future;
3. Attitudes about the present, why the present range of attitudes exists, and how these attitudes may change in the future;
4. Values upon which the present has been built, the values each of us chooses to claim as our own, and the role of values in determining the future, which is created by our actions today.

In 1971 the University of Minnesota established the Office for Applied Social Science and the Future within its Center for Urban and Regional Affairs. The office successfully introduced a future-orientation into many sectors of the university. The College of Liberal Arts offers an undergraduate social science major in future studies, leading to a bachelor of elective studies degree. Students in the program may choose from among more than 30 courses in at least 10 departments. In addition, the college offers an extensive series of quarterly seminars in alternative futures. In the College of Education, many undergraduate courses have been restructured to emphasize alternative social and educational futures. At the graduate level, the college offers a program in alternative and educational futures as one of five possible fields of concentration leading to the master's and doctoral degrees.

The University of Houston in Clear Lake City, Texas, has two degree programs in futures research: one general, the other in education. Houston-Clear Lake, which opened in 1974, has implemented a fairly innovative approach to higher education. The curriculum of the university, an upper-level institution admitting juniors, seniors, and graduate students, is not organized around traditional academic departments but rather around program areas such as individual and social behavior, multicultural studies, resource utilization, and studies of the future. Candidates pursuing a 36-hour master of science degree in studies of the future may construct their programs from 20-odd futures courses and from courses offered by other university programs. The futures courses include forecasting techniques, educational futuristics, public policy, technology, and apocalyptic images.

The above are a few examples that illustrate how futuristics can be implemented at different levels of education. Futurists generally agree on the approaches needed to implement a future-oriented curriculum. First, they suggest a reevaluation of current course offerings in light of current needs, interests, and potential problems. Second, they recommend an interdisciplinary approach to help students realize that solutions to future problems are not always found within only one field of study. Third, futurists urge educators to make greater use of the methods and outlooks of futuristics, such as those described in the previous chapter. These suggestions can improve the linkage between contemporary schooling and our students' lives in the years ahead. As H. G. Wells once stated, "Human history becomes more and more a race between education and catastrophe." Hopefully, through future-oriented education, we can avoid catastrophe.

Bibliography

Bart, Pauline B. "Why Women See the Future Differently from Men." In *Learning for Tomorrow*, edited by Alvin Toffler, New York: Vintage Books, 1974.

Cornish, Edward. *The Study of the Future*. Washington, D.C.: World Future Society, 1977.

Ehrlich, Paul. "Eco-Catastrophe!" In *The Futurists*, edited by Alvin Toffler. New York: Random House, 1972.

"Faculty Forecasting Through History." *The Futurist* (December, 1968): 121.

Glenn, Jerry, and Guy, Cyndy. "Easy Ways To Help Children Think About the Future." *The Futurist* (August, 1974): 186-88.

Gordon, Theodore J. "The Current Methods of Futures Research." In *The Futurists*, edited by Alvin Toffler. New York: Random House, 1972.

Heyman, Mark. *Simulation Games for the Classroom*. Bloomington, Indiana: Phi Delta Kappa Educational Foundation, 1975.

Hollister, Bernard C., and Thompson, Deane C. *Grokking the Future*. Pflaum/Standard, 1973.

Kauffman, Draper L., Jr. *Futurism and Future Studies*. Washington, D.C.: National Education Association, 1976.

_____ . *Teaching the Future*. Palm Springs, California: ETC Publications, 1976.

LaConte, Ronald T. *Teaching Tomorrow Today*. New York: Bantam Books, Inc., 1975.

Poussaint, Alvin F. "The Black Child's Image of the Future." In *Learning for Tomorrow*, edited by Alvin Toffler. New York: Vintage Books, 1974.

Shane, Harold G. *The Educational Significance of the Future*. Bloomington, Indiana: Phi Delta Kappa, Inc., 1973.

Singer, Benjamin D. "The Future-Focused Role-Image." In *Learning for Tomorrow*, edited by Alvin Toffler. New York, Vintage Books, 1974.

Stirewalt, James. "The Future as an Academic Subject." *World Future Society Bulletin* (January-February, 1977): 16-20.

_____ . "The Future as an Academic Subject—Part II." *World Future Society Bulletin* (March-April, 1977): 9-14.

Toffler, Alvin. *Future Shock*. New York: Random House, 1970.

_____ . "The Psychology of the Future." In *Learning for Tomorrow*, edited by Alvin Toffler. New York: Vintage Books, 1974.

Ziegler, Warren L. *Social and Technological Developments*. Syracuse, New York: Educational Policy Research Center, 1971.

Fastback Titles *(continued from back cover)*

Single copies of fastbacks are 75¢ (60¢ to Phi Delta Kappa members). Write to Phi Delta Kappa, Eighth and Union, Box 789, Bloomington, IN 47402 for quantity discounts for any title or combination of titles.

PDK Fastback Series Titles

(Continued on inside back cover)

See inside back cover for prices.